UNDERCOVER
GOLF

An Off-the-Links Guide
to Improving
Your Game—
at Work, at Home,
and on the Sly

UNDERCOVER GOLF

**An Off-the-Links Guide
to Improving
Your Game—
at Work, at Home,
and on the Sly**

By JOE BORGENICHT
with R. D. ROBINSON

QUIRK BOOKS
PHILADELPHIA

Copyright © 2004 by Quirk Productions, Inc.

All rights reserved. No part of this book may be reproduced
in any form without written permission from the publisher.

Library of Congress Cataloging-in-Publication Number:
2003095960

ISBN: 1-931686-72-6

Printed in Singapore

Typeset in HelveticaNeue

Designed by Michael Rogalski

Illustrations by Dan Krovatin

Edited by Erin Slonaker

Distributed in North America by Chronicle Books
85 Second Street
San Francisco, CA 94105

10 9 8 7 6 5 4 3 2 1

Quirk Books
215 Church Street
Philadelphia, PA 19106

www.quirkbooks.com

CONTENTS

INTRODUCTION

Eighteen holes is never enough.

Even if you've finished a round feeling soundly balanced, stretched, and fulfilled—with a score under 90—you'll want to do better. Sometimes you finish your round with the memory of one particular stroke—out of the 105 you took—etched into your mind, and you want nothing more than to figure out what went wrong and fix it. It is not a question of whether you golf; it is a question of when you can do it again.

Unfortunately for most of us, golfing every day is not at option. Minor responsibilities such as work, errands, and family constantly compete with our golf time. Golf has the ability to steal husbands from wives, fathers from children, and employees from work.

That's where this book comes in. *Undercover Golf* is a very simple program designed to allow you to develop your fundamentals anytime, anywhere without shirking responsibility. Each chapter is broken down by fundamental skill: grip, aim and setup, backswing motion, downswing motion and finish, and putting. The positions, postures, and motions defined by each fundamental have then been matched with a similar position, posture, or motion that you already use to perform common daily activities. This practice will allow you to train your golf fundamentals under the guise of performing other non-golf responsibilities and chores.

In other words, you'll get credit for helping out around the house, running errands, or staying focused at work while you secretly train your golf swing for a repeatable and reliable motion.

At work you can check your hand position while looking interested at the weekly budgeting meeting. You'll learn to practice your posture while talking to a coworker in his or her office, to check your arm position while adjusting an overhead desk lamp, and more.

At home you will learn how to grip the club with your right hand while hanging freshly laundered shirts. Your right-hand grip will become habit and your significant other will be pleased that you are keeping up with your laundry. Mopping the floor will no longer be a tiresome chore; it becomes a training session to practice taking your club back along the target line.

Out shopping? Now those long waits holding bags while your significant other is in the dressing room provide valuable time to practice your putting stroke. Boring dinner dates will be less painful when you take a moment to train proper knee pressure. Later, you can excuse yourself to the restroom to wash your hands and check your alignment to the target.

If you are a newcomer to golf, we recommend that you read and practice the skills in this book from beginning to end. You'll be better off if you develop consistent fundamentals and proper undercover habits early on.

Additionally, the less obsessed you appear at first, the easier it will be to get out for a round of golf or time on the practice tee.

If you have been golfing for some time, your task is a bit more complicated. Since you are likely to have golf widows, orphans, and very few personal days left on your roster, we recommend that you go deep undercover using one of two methods:

Method A. Select the fundamentals appropriate to your skill level and work on training those skills, finding excuses to take on the everyday tasks outlined in the book.

Method B. Select the chore, task, or errand that will earn you the most credit in the eyes of your boss, significant other, or child, and then perform the accompanying skill.

Advanced golfers may find that the positions described in these fundamentals differ slightly from their own motion. In such cases, adjust the instructions to match your developed posture, position, or motion.

Whether you are hitting them right all day and putting like there's no tomorrow or your day is spent duffing from the left to the right, we think you'll agree: eighteen holes is never enough.

NOTE: All directions in this book are given for a right-handed golfer. A left-handed golfer must swap right for left and vice versa for the exercises in the book.

CHAPTER 1

GRIP

PROPER GRIP

Your grip on the club is the most important part of your golf swing. As your only physical link to the club, it is the key to your swing. Your ability to direct the ball is greatly improved with a proper grip. After all, you wouldn't build a house on a foundation of sand; do not establish a golf swing on a faulty grip.

An incorrect grip will cause the clubhead to come out of alignment with the target line on both back- and downswings. Additionally, you will tend to adjust your body and swing motion to compensate for faulty hand placement.

A grip that is too tight, too strong, or too weak will negatively affect the direction and flight of the ball. Squeezing the club too tightly creates tension in your hands, wrists, and arms and results in a staccato swing and restricted ball flight. A so-called "strong" grip—when your hands are too far under the club to the right— guarantees a closed clubface at impact and a hooked shot. A so-called "weak" grip—when your hands are on top of the club—will guarantee an open clubface at impact and a sliced shot.

Of course, the golf course is the last place to practice your golf grip. You should arrive on the first tee already confident that your grip is sound. Develop a reliable grip while hanging clothes, while attending a meeting at your

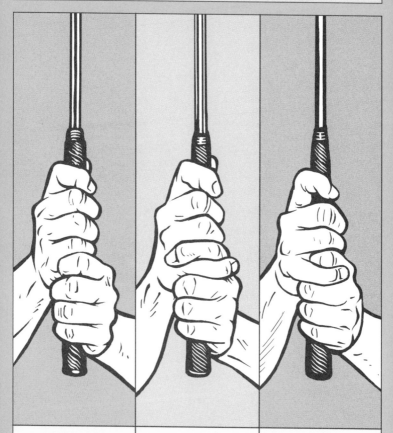

Proper Grip

Ten-Finger Grip: Right pinkie rests against index finger of left hand.

Interlocking Grip: Right pinkie interlocks with index finger of left hand.

Overlapping Grip: Right pinkie rests atop the index finger of the left hand.

office, or while stuck in traffic. Training your grip off-course will teach you to hold the club fittingly and to set your body correctly when you are on the links.

Review the following fundamentals of grip. Practice the scenarios in this chapter whenever you find yourself cleaning up, measuring, shoveling, or daydreaming in a work meeting. By the time you are through practicing and fulfilling your responsibilities, your significant other or roommate will be happy, your coworkers will be tended to, and you will be gripping a golf club as if your hands were sculpted around it.

Correct Grip Goals

- To connect to the club with little or no tension in your hands, wrists, and arms.

- To connect to the club in a natural position with a natural pressure.

Correct Grip Elements

- Left hand clamps the club in place.

  Club is locked between the last three fingers and the meaty pad where your left hand connects to your wrist on the pinkie side.

  Left thumb and forefinger are pressed together at the base of the forefinger and joint of the thumb.

  Left thumb rides down the right side of the club.

Left forefinger wraps under the club.

- Right hand is positioned to direct the ball.

  Right middle and ring fingers are under the shaft of the club.

  Right thumb and forefinger are pressed together at the base of the forefinger and first joint of the thumb.

  "Valley" of right hand is folded over the left thumb.

  Right forefinger wraps under the club.

  Right pinkie may overlap, interlock, or rest against the forefinger of the left hand.

- Left and right hands work together as one.

- Full grip pressure is soft enough to feel the weight of the clubhead.

- Hands and forearms hang naturally.

TRAINING YOUR RIGHT-HAND GRIP WHILE HANGING SHIRTS

The Cover: You are hanging freshly laundered dress shirts in your closet.

The Objective: To correctly set your right hand.

Do not attempt to train your right-hand grip using unbendable plastic hangers or while hanging pants.

The Gear:
- Six or seven wire hangers
- An equal number of button-style shirts

The Technique:
Step 1. Prepare one of the hangers.

Press the center of the hanger's horizontal bar up toward the base of the hook. This will form two wings about 1 1/2 to 2 inches (3.8–5 cm) wide, one of which will serve as your club. (Additionally, the newly rounded corners of the hanger will eliminate visible hanger points on the shoulders of shirts that are not worn frequently.)

Step 2. Place the lower bar of the hanger across your open right hand.

With your palm facing up and your hand flat, place the hanger so that it runs diagonally across your fingers— from the base of your pinkie to the top of the middle joint of your index finger.

Grip a modified wire hanger as if it is your golf club, being sure to place the "V" of your index finger and thumb along the top wire. Hang your freshly ironed shirt and move on to the next; you'll have a closetful of crisp shirts and a reliable right-hand grip in no time.

Step 3. Squeeze your right thumb and forefinger together.

Prepare your right hand by pressing from the base of your thumb and align your thumb and index finger so that the middle joint of your thumb touches the side of your index knuckle. Notice the small "V" formed between the pad of your thumb and your forefinger, with the base of the "V" at the point where the two come together (at the joints).

Step 4. Grip the hanger.

Curl your fingers up and fold your thumb over the top of the hanger so that the top wire runs directly up the middle of the "V" described above. The top wire of the hanger should be running into the "V" formed in the palm of your hand—between the meaty pads at the bases of your thumb and pinkie. Use your left hand to shake out the shirt you are going to hang.

Step 5. Adjust your grip pressure points and insert the left arm of the hanger into a shirt sleeve.

Press up on the bottom wire using your ring and middle fingers, while simultaneously pressing down from the base of the "V." Note that these are the pressure points with which you will hold your golf club with your right hand.

Step 6. Release your grip and complete hanging the shirt.

Step 7. Repeat Steps 1 through 6 until all of your shirts are hung or your right-hand grip is instinctive.

TRAINING YOUR LEFT-HAND GRIP WHILE STUCK IN TRAFFIC

The Cover: You are patiently sitting in your unmoving car, maintaining your hands in the correct driving position.

The Objective: To train your left-hand grip.

Due to the hazards of doing anything other than driving while you are driving, it is recommended that you only practice your left-hand grip while stopped in traffic, at a stop light, or parked in the driveway waiting for a friend, associate, or golf partner. Once you have mastered your left-hand grip on the steering wheel, you may use your grip to control the wheel—however, you should continue to focus on the road.

The Setting:
• A stoplight or traffic jam

The Gear:
• A car steering wheel

The Technique:
Step 1. Place your left hand behind the steering wheel.

With your hand flat and your palm facing you, set your left hand behind the wheel at about 10 o'clock, fingers aimed to the right and thumb straight up. With the wheel set between the base and first joint of your index finger, the natural curve of the wheel will align properly to your finger grip, spanning the base of your index

While the light is red, set your left hand in place around the steering wheel, with your last three fingers tucked around.

Squeeze your thumb and forefinger together and fold your thumb over the steering wheel. When the light turns green, you will be prepared to confidently steer your car.

finger to the callous pad of your pinkie. This mimics the
club's placement in a proper left-hand grip. Check to
see whether traffic is moving yet.

Step 2. Close your last three fingers around the steering wheel.

Curl your pinkie, ring, and middle fingers around the
steering wheel. Ensure that your grasp is in your fingers
and not your palm. Your thumb and forefinger should
remain off the wheel, naturally forming a "trigger finger"
position.

Step 3. Squeeze your left thumb and forefinger together.

Press from the base of your thumb and align your
thumb and index finger so that the middle joint of your
thumb touches the side of your index knuckle. Notice
the "V" formed between the pad of your thumb and
your forefinger, with the base of the "V" at the point
where the two come together.

Step 4. Fold your thumb over the steering wheel so
that it rests on the inside of the wheel.

Let your index finger close naturally around the wheel.
Your hand should now be placed as if it were around a
club.

Step 5. Adjust your grip pressure points.

Press the wheel between your bottom three fingers and

the meaty pad (pinkie side) at the base of your hand—about an inch (2.5 cm) above where your hand connects to your wrist. Note that the base of your three fingers and the pad are the pressure points with which you will hold your golf club with your left hand. Continue to grip and control the steering wheel with your left hand as you inch forward in traffic.

Step 6. Feel the grip for about 1 minute, then release. Repeat Steps 1 through 5 until the light changes, traffic clears, or your left-hand grip is instinctive.

CHECKING FULL GRIP WHILE USING A MEASURING STICK

The Cover: You are tackling a home-improvement project that involves measuring.

The Objective: To check your full grip.

This procedure may be executed with either a yard- or meter-long measuring stick or a short ruler. Choose the appropriate tool for your "extra" endeavor. For example, if you are sitting at a desk, use a ruler rather than a measuring stick. If you are measuring a large room, use a measuring stick rather than a ruler.

The Gear:
• A yard- or meter-long measuring stick or a ruler
  (12 in/30 cm minimum)

• Athletic or duct tape

The Technique:
Step 1. Prepare the measuring stick.

Wrap tape around at least 8 inches (20 cm) of one end of the measuring tool to simulate the grip on the club.

Step 2. Place one narrow edge of the tool in your left hand.

Lay the stick diagonally across the base of your last three fingers and between the base and middle joints of your index finger so that 3 inches (7.5 cm) of the stick extend past your pinkie.

Step 3. Curl your last three fingers around the measuring stick.

Step 4. Press the inside edge of your thumb and forefinger together and fold your hand over the top of the measuring stick or ruler.

Squeeze the first joint of your thumb into the pad at the base of your forefinger. Fold your hand over the top of the stick so that the meaty pad at the base of your hand on the pinkie side rests on top of the tool. Your thumb should be running down the right side of the stick and your forefinger should be wrapped under the stick.

Step 5. Place the measuring stick across the base of your right middle two fingers.

Set the measuring stick in place on your right hand so that your two hands are nearly touching.

Step 6. Interlock or overlap your right pinkie with your left forefinger.

Slide your right hand closer to your left so that your right ring finger and left forefinger are touching. Alternatively, set your right hand so that only your right pinkie touches the left forefinger (this is called a ten-finger grip).

Step 7. Curl your middle and ring fingers around the yard stick or ruler.

Gripping a measuring stick with your left hand as if it is your club places you in a perfect position to measure windows for drapes.

Step 8. Press your right thumb and forefinger together and fold your hand over the top of the measuring tool.

Squeeze the first joint of your thumb into the pad at the base of your forefinger. Fold your right hand over the top of the stick so that your left thumb fits into the valley of your right palm. Your right thumb should run down the left side of the stick and your forefinger should be wrapped under the stick.

Step 9. Hold the measuring stick as you take your measurements of, say, a picture window.

Feel the marriage of your two hands on the tool. They should feel as one. Maintain this grip as you measure all dimensions of the window.

CHECKING PROPER GRIP PRESSURE WHILE SHOVELING

The Cover: You are clearing snow from your driveway or are preparing a garden bed.

The Objective: To ensure you are exerting the correct amount of pressure in your grip.

The following technique is best for loosely packed snow, dirt, or sand. Secretly hone your grip pressure while shoveling, whether you're clearing snow, turning topsoil, or digging a sand castle's moat.

The Gear:
• A shovel appropriate for your conditions

• A pile of snow, sand, or loose dirt

The Technique:
Step 1. Grip the shovel.

Grip the handle of the shovel about 3 inches (7–8 cm) down from the end. Use as near a full grip as possible. (This may be slightly difficult, as the shaft will be wider than the shaft of a bent hanger, steering wheel, measuring stick, or golf club.) Focus on holding the shovel using the pressure points described in the training skills on pages 17 and 21. If you are shoveling for a spouse or significant other, be sure that he or she sees you grasping the shovel and preparing for work.

While gripping the shovel, test the weight of the shovel head and note how your grip pressure adjusts to compensate. While clearing your path of snow, practice using a consistent grip pressure so that the motion is smooth and effortless.

Step 2. Feel the weight of the shovel head and adjust your grip pressure accordingly.

Hold the shovel head about 3 inches (7–8 cm) off the ground. Bend your wrists slightly up and down to feel the weight of the shovel head. If you cannot feel the weight of the shovel head, loosen your grip pressure. If the shovel head drops to the ground, tighten your grip pressure. Correct grip pressure will allow you to hold the shovel about 3 inches (7–8 cm) off the ground and to control its vertical movement. This is equivalent to feeling the clubhead when gripping your club on the links.

Step 3. Draw the shovel back into position to shovel.

As you pull the shovel back, notice that your grip pressure naturally tightens slightly. The same adjustment occurs with your golf swing. Prepare to shovel by bending your knees and straightening your back.

Step 4. Dig into the snow, dirt, or sand at an angle of approximately 30 degrees and adjust your grip pressure accordingly.

If the shovel pushes through too quickly, then your grip pressure may be too tight. If the shovel slips out of your hands, then your grip pressure is too loose. Note that your grip pressure will vary depending on the density of the material you are shoveling. Similarly, your grip pressure on the links will vary based on the surface on which the ball lies.

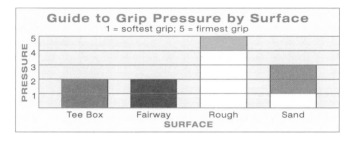

Step 5. Repeat Steps 1 through 4 until your pile is shoveled and correct grip pressure is instinctual.

CHECKING PROPER HAND POSITION IN A MEETING

The Cover: You are attending a meeting around the conference table at the office.

The Objective: To practice proper hand position.

All too often on the golf course, you may find yourself anxiously shifting your grip just before swinging the club. These nervous and hesitant actions will inevitably send your ball on a faulty trajectory. Rather than question your hand position on the links, train and check it while in work situations.

The Gear:
- A pen or a pencil
- A chair
- A table

The Technique:
Step 1. Grip the pen or pencil in your left hand.

Lay the pen across the base of your last three fingers. Curl those fingers under the pen, press the joint of your thumb into the pad at the base of your index finger, and close your grip over the pen, curling your index finger under the pen. Note the "V" formed at the base of your thumb and index finger. Your thumb runs down the right side of the pen.

Check that your left-hand grip is accurate by bringing the pen to your lips briefly. Your coworkers will believe you are concentrating.

Square your shoulders, extend your left arm, and bevel your wrist to check that the line running from the base of your thumb and forefinger points to your right shoulder.

Maintain your left-hand grip as you place the pen under the table and grip the pen with both hands. Adjust your right-hand grip to the proper position, keeping both arms straight.

Step 2. Bring the instrument briefly to your lips to indicate your concentration on the meeting at hand; furrow your brow for added emphasis.

Step 3. Adjust your left-hand grip to the proper position. Extend your left arm straight out in front of you and set your hand on the table so that it is centered in front of your body.

Step 4. Sit back in your chair and square your shoulders. Check that the line running from the base of your thumb and forefinger points to your right shoulder.

Step 5. Relax your expression and check that no one is waiting for you to say anything. Adjust your left hand "V" and speak if necessary.

Step 6. Retract your arm and grip the pen or pencil with your right hand. Maintaining your left-hand grip, lay the pen across the base of your right middle and ring fingers, interlock or overlap your right pinkie with your left forefinger, and press the joint of your thumb into the pad at the base of your index finger. Curl your ring and middle fingers around the instrument and fold your right hand over your left thumb so that your left thumb fits into the valley of your right palm. Note the "V" formed at the base of your thumb and index finger.

Step 7. Adjust your right-hand grip to the proper position.

Extend your arms straight out in front of you beneath the table. Let your right elbow bend slightly toward your right hip. Sit back in your chair and square your shoulders. Check that the point of the "V" is aimed at your right shoulder. Adjust if necessary.

Step 8. Release your grip and join the meeting.

Speak only as long as necessary, then repeat Steps 1 through 4 until your hand placement is consistent and/or the meeting comes to a close.

CHAPTER 2

AIM AND SETUP

PROPER AIM AND SETUP

Correct aim and setup are vital for executing an accurate swing—perhaps as important as the swing motion itself. Imagine trying to drive your car down the highway with your wheels out of alignment. You'll be making corrections the entire trip rather than cruising down the interstate.

Establishing correct aim at home, in your office, or while running errands will help you to trust your swing and to eliminate "swing thoughts"—those nagging doubts you develop in the middle of your swing. Establishing correct setup will allow your body to naturally perform a repeatable and reliable swing motion.

As a rule, the ball will go where you aim it—grip and swing motion aside. If you are not aimed correctly, however, the ball will never obey your wishes. Golfing with faulty aim may lead you to make unnecessary adjustments in your swing rather than simply correcting your body to the target line.

If your setup is correct, your position will allow your body to naturally execute an accurate swing. If your setup is incorrect, your body will be prohibited from performing a fluid and correct swing motion. For example, if you set up with your hips open to the target line—rather than square to it—you will not be able to turn as far as you should. On the downswing, you may clear your hips too far to the left, which will cause you to open the club-

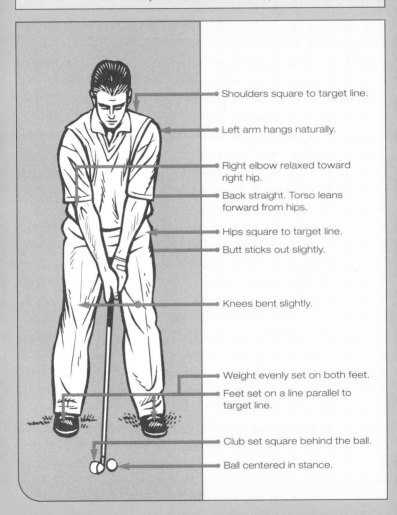

Shoulders square to target line.

Left arm hangs naturally.

Right elbow relaxed toward right hip.

Back straight. Torso leans forward from hips.

Hips square to target line.

Butt sticks out slightly.

Knees bent slightly.

Weight evenly set on both feet.

Feet set on a line parallel to target line.

Club set square behind the ball.

Ball centered in stance.

face on impact, thereby slicing the ball.

The basics of correct aim and setup that follow are not new—you have surely heard them numerous times before—but they'll help you reconsider the fundamentals. Check your own on-course routine against the following simple off-course instructions and make any adjustments to your own process as necessary. Repeat the checks until your own aim and setup routine becomes habit.

Aim and Setup Goals

- To assume an athletic position in your posture prior to making your swing motion.

- To trust that the ball and your body are aligned correctly to the target, eliminating needless worries.

Aim and Setup Elements

- Ball should be aimed to a specific target.

- Club should be set square behind the ball.

- Feet should be perpendicular to the target line (the imaginary line running from the ball to the target), and along a line parallel to the target line.

- Feet should be set about shoulder-width apart.

- Ball should be centered in stance.

- Hips should be square to the target line (parallel with the line).

- Shoulders should be square to the target line (parallel
  with the line).

  Left arm should hang naturally to bring left shoulder
  square with the target line.

  Relax right elbow toward right hip to bring shoulders
  to square.

- Back should be straight.
- Butt should stick out slightly.
- Torso should lean forward from the hips.
- Knees should be relaxed or bent slightly.
- Weight should be evenly set on balls of both feet.

PICKING YOUR TARGET AND JUDGING DISTANCE WHILE TAKING A WALK

The Cover: You are taking your dog out for her daily walk or joining your loved ones in a leisurely stroll.

The Objective: To pick your target and judge its distance from you.

Rather than being aimed in a general direction toward the green or the pin, your ball should be aimed at a specific landing zone, a circle a few yards (or meters) in diameter. Practice selecting a target and judging your distance to that target while on a walk—your off-course loved ones will be tended to and your on-course golf balls will be better placed.

The Setting:
• A place to walk (roughly 100–300 yards/90–270 meters long)

The Gear:
• A significant other, child, or dog (all optional)

The Technique:
Step 1. Casually come to a stop and select a "ball."

While pretending to admire the scenery (or waiting for your dog), find an object in your path—a pebble, piece of bark, stuck gum, or the like. This will be your first "ball."

Step 2. Facing the direction you will be walking, stand a few steps behind your "ball" and select a target.

Choose a tree, building, parked car, or other landmark toward which you can walk in an unimpeded, straight line. The target should be no more than two standard city blocks away.

Step 3. Pick a landing zone.

Imagine a circular landing zone a few yards (or meters) in diameter around your target. The farther away your target, the larger your landing zone should be.

Step 4. Estimate the distance from your "ball" to your landing zone.

On hills and variable terrain, judge distance by drawing an imaginary straight line from your "ball" to your target. Avoid using parked cars, homes, or sidewalk squares—objects of easily determined length—to help your estimation, as these tools will not be available on the golf course. Make a guess by estimating how many times a 6-foot (2-meter) tall man could lie down between the two points, then calculating the total distance.

Step 5. Walk straight to your target, counting your steps as you go.

Keep your eyes fixed on your landing zone. If you are walking on a crowded street—or your dog, child, or

Select a target and landing zone in the distance and try to guess how far away they are. Count how many steps it takes to reach it, and calculate the distance to see how good your guess was. With practice, gauging distance will become second nature.

loved one needs to detour for a moment—remember where you left the path, how many steps you have taken, and resume your count from that point.

Step 6. Visualize your shot.

See your ball's flight, path, and trajectory in your mind. If there are trees in the way, imagine what type of shot you would need to hit to clear the trees.

Step 7. When you reach your landing zone, note the number of steps you walked.

Multiply this number by your stride length. Compare the result with your estimated distance. The closer your estimate is to the actual distance, the better your powers of judging distance.

Step 8. Repeat Steps 1 through 6 from your landing zone to a new location.

Vary distances and landing zones as you walk.

Determining Stride Length

If you do not know the approximate length of your stride, use the following procedure:

- Mark a point "A" on the ground with a stone.

- Use a tape measure to measure exactly 20 feet (6 meters) from that point and mark it "B" with a second stone.

- Beginning with your toes on point A, stride naturally to point B—counting steps as you walk.

- Continue to walk through point B (do not adjust your stride to end exactly at point B).

- Determine how many steps you took to arrive at point B.

- Divide 20 feet (or 6 meters) by the number of steps you took.

- The result is your stride length, which should be roughly between 2 and 3 feet ($2/3$ and 1 meter) per stride.

ALIGNING TO THE TARGET
WHILE WAITING IN LINE

The Cover: You are patiently standing in any line.

The Objective: To properly align to the target.

Whether waiting for the foursome ahead of you to clear the green or waiting in line at the store, movie theater, or back-nine snack bar, you must always stay aligned to your target. This will ensure that your target line is accurately aimed to your landing zone on the course.

The Setting:
• A line to stand in (preferably slow moving)

The Technique:

Step 1. Step into line.

Step 2. Pick a target.

Choose a non-moving target that is in front of you as you face the front of the line. If you are outside, choose a target at least 30 yards (27 m) away—a stop sign, parking meter, or theater box office. In smaller spaces or indoors, select a target as far away as the space allows.

Step 3. Facing your target, imagine a ball in front of your feet.

Put your feet side by side, aiming toward your target. Select a stationary object or floor marking 2 or 3 inches (5–8 cm) in front of your feet. This will be your "ball."

Step 4. Look up from your "ball" toward your target.

As you slowly look up, draw an imaginary line from your "ball" to your target. If it intersects with any other patrons in line, signage, or other objects, learn to ignore them. (When you move forward in line, select new "balls" along the same target line.)

Step 5. Focus on your line.

Visualize the path your "ball" will have to travel along this line to help you "see" it. (Do not stare at other patrons in line—it's rude.)

Step 6. Casually sway from side to side as you hold your focus on your line.

With your feet firmly planted, nonchalantly sway from side to side. Note how the patrons and your environment move around your line. Notice how a slight shift to the left or the right of your target would send your "ball" farther to the right or left, respectively, of your target.

Step 7. Take a half-step to the left of your ball and pivot your body so that it is parallel to your target line.

Stay focused on your line and note how your new position alters your perspective. Be sure that you are square to the line and that the patrons behind you do not think you are stepping out of line now that you are no longer facing the front.

Aligning to the Target While Waiting in Line

Stand facing your target and visualize your target line.

Take your stance parallel to the target line and look at it again to ensure you are aligned properly.

Step 8. Step forward in line as it moves, repeating Steps 1 through 7 until you can confidently align with a target or you reach the front of the line.

PRACTICING PARALLEL SETUP WHILE CLIMBING STAIRS

The Cover: You are committing yourself to healthier living by taking the stairs instead of the elevator.

The Objective: To make sure your setup is correct.

A good golf swing requires that your feet, hips, and shoulders are all square to the target line. You can practice your setup while climbing stairs—just as long as the staircase is not spiral, which might result in a fade or drawn shot. For a healthy heart and a healthier setup, take your golf alignment to the stairs every day.

The Setting:
• A staircase of at least three steps

The Technique:
Step 1. Step up one step.

Stand on the step with both feet facing forward.

Step 2. Set your toes against the riser of the next step.

Stand in the center of the step with your feet roughly shoulder-width apart. Note that this is the position you will use on the golf course to set your feet squarely to the target line. Check behind you to be sure that no one is trying to pass you on the stairs.

Step 3. Square your hips to the step below.

Use the same line that your toes are on as a reference point. If your hips are square to this line, your knees will be parallel to it as well. Look down to check if you're parallel and adjust accordingly.

Step 4. Lean forward at the hips and bend your knees slightly.

Step 5. Square your shoulders to the line of the step.

Let your hands hang freely at your sides (your palms will be facing your thighs). Bring your shoulders to square with your reference line. Look down to check if you're parallel and adjust accordingly.

Step 6. Repeat Steps 1 through 5 on each successive step until you reach the top of the stairs or your parallel setup is instinctual.

Be sure that you are clear of anyone going up or coming down the stairs.

Step up onto the first step, placing your toes into the rise of the stair. Check the crowd to see if anyone is watching you.

Lean forward at the hips and bend your knees to assume an athletic posture. Square your shoulders to the step and hold for a moment. Repeat on the next step.

TRAINING YOUR AIM
AND SETUP WHILE
WASHING YOUR HANDS

The Cover: You are cleaning germs from your hands before a meal or after using the restroom.

The Objective: To train your aim and setup until they are instinctual.

Simple bathroom details (the line of the tiles, the drain in the sink) are convenient elements you can use to simulate your target line and ball. Hold the position of each step so that you can feel how each new adjustment resets your position.

The Gear:
- A sink with a flat top and square front
- A paper towel folded to a point (like the nose of a paper airplane)
- A tile or linoleum floor, or a throw rug

The Technique:
Step 1. Step up to the sink.

Stand so that your hips (or thighs) touch the edge of the sink.

Step 2. Look down at the drain—this will be your "ball."

Step 3. Pick a target and aim your "ball."

Look to your left and draw an imaginary straight line running from the drain directly to your specific target (a hand dryer or towel rack). This will be your "target line." Your target line will run parallel to the edge of the sink and your hips.

Step 4. Lay the folded paper towel to the right of your "ball."

Lay the paper towel so that the arrow points at the target. Ensure that the paper towel is parallel to the edge of the sink closest to you.

Step 5. Establish a stance line parallel to your target line.

Choose a line in the floor tile or linoleum that runs parallel to the target line. Alternatively, set the edge of a throw rug parallel to your target line. This will be your stance line.

Don't worry needlessly about incorrect alignment. The paper towel and the edge of the sink are aligned correctly. Trust that and let go of any doubts, which will otherwise inhibit your swing on the course.

Use both a folded paper towel aimed at the drain and the tiles in the floor to help you align to the ball. Keeping your body square to these lines will help you keep your body square to the target line on the course.

Step 6. Address the drain and set your feet to the target line.

Face your target line. Center the drain in your stance. Set your feet—about shoulder-width apart—so that the tips of your shoes touch your stance line. You may place your toes either square to the line or with the toes of your left foot aimed slightly toward your target—as long as the tips of both feet touch the same target line.

Step 7. Square your hips to the target line.

Hold your feet in place as you set your hips parallel to your target line. If your left foot is slightly open—toward the target—you may need to kick your left hip slightly toward the ball. Use the front edge of the sink as a reference, as this line will be parallel to both your target and stance lines.

Step 8. Lean forward from the hips.

With a straight back, stick your butt out slightly and lean forward toward the drain.

Step 9. Relax your knees slightly.

Lower yourself slightly by bending at the knees. You should feel your weight, evenly balanced from foot to foot, settle on the inside balls of your feet.

Step 10. Turn on the water in the sink.

Adjust to a comfortable temperature.

Step 11. Put your hands under the water and square your shoulders to the target line.

Pretend to grip a club with both hands—this will extend them under the water, just above the drain. Your left shoulder should be higher than your right and slightly open to the target line. Relax your right elbow slightly toward your right hip. This will bring your shoulders into parallel with your hips, feet, and target line—and allow you to wash the back of your left hand and the palm of your right.

Step 12. Continue to wash your hands, checking your setup and alignment as necessary.

Turn off the faucets to conserve water as you restart your alignment process.

PRACTICING YOUR POSTURE WHILE TALKING TO A COWORKER

The Cover: You are conducting a one-on-one conversation in your or a coworker's office.

The Objective: To practice your golfing posture.

All too often, you may find yourself standing over the ball at the tee box wondering if you are standing too close or too far from the ball. Your ability to finish in a balanced position relies solely on your ability to start from a balanced position. Use the following technique to both review your swing posture and appear attentive to the discussion at hand. You must be able to remain standing but not look out of place during the entire conversation.

The Gear:
- A desk or piece of office furniture about hip high
- A coworker

The Technique:
Step 1. Find an appropriate position in your coworker's office.

Position yourself facing your coworker so that your imaginary "ball" is between you and her. Be sure that you have a desk or short filing cabinet behind you.

Step 2. Visualize a target line.

Pick a location for the "ball" about a yard (1 meter) in front of you and visualize a target line for it. (You don't necessarily need a target for this exercise, just a ball on a line you can square yourself to.)

Step 3. Set up your feet and look down.

Look down at your feet and set them so that they are perpendicular to the line. This will serve two purposes: You will be able to correctly spot and set up your stance parallel to the imaginary target line, and you will show your coworker that you are mentally preparing yourself for your talk.

Step 4. Square your hips and look at your coworker.

Square your hips so that they are parallel to the target line. If you cannot perform this move naturally, slide your hands into your pockets or onto your hips and make eye contact at the same time you make your move.

Step 5. Straighten your back and pretend to take an interest in what your coworker is saying.

Straighten from your butt to the top of your head. This upright posture will also make you appear attentive.

Pick a location for your ball and visualize the target line. Place your hands in your pockets to help you square your hips to the target line.

Pretend to be listening as you straighten your back. Maintain this athletic posture.

Stick out your butt, lean forward from the hips, and lower yourself onto the file cabinet.

Step 6. Slightly stick out your butt while conversing.

Momentarily focus on what your coworker is saying and respond appropriately. Stick out your butt slightly as you nod or shake your head. The motion of your head (and any verbal response you may offer) may distract her from the fact that you are sticking out your butt.

Step 7. Lean forward from the hips as if you are about to speak.

Lean your torso slightly forward. Bend from the hips. It should appear as though you are about to interject something, but then check yourself—move hastily to Step 8 before you speak.

Step 8. Lower yourself into position on the edge of the desk or filing cabinet behind you.

Bend your knees to settle into the proper and complete golf-swing posture. Be sure that as you lower yourself, your weight falls onto the balls of your feet. Wiggle your toes to confirm this. Perching on the edge of the desk or cabinet will indicate that you are ready both to focus on whatever your coworker is saying and—most importantly—to swing from a squared and balanced position.

PRACTICING PROPER WEIGHT DISTRIBUTION WHILE DRINKING AT A BAR

The Cover: You are casually and confidently standing at a bar with a drink.

The Objective: To assume an athletic posture and practice proper weight distribution.

Setting yourself into a natural, athletic position will make you comfortable and at ease at a bar or on the tee. Properly distributing your weight on your feet will give you this confident stance. Whether at the bar or on the links, it'll help you score.

The Gear:
• A hip-high bar stool

The Technique:
Step 1. Set yourself up at the bar.

Stand facing the bar or at a high table. Set a hip-high bar stool directly behind you and order a drink.

Step 2. Set yourself up in front of the bar stool.

Stand just a few inches (several centimeters) in front of the bar stool. Place your feet about shoulder-width apart so that your toes are on a line parallel to the bar or, if the bar or table is curved, to the stool. Look down briefly to check your feet—you can also reach into your pocket or bag and pull out your wallet at this point.

While in an athletic posture, lean forward from the hips and reach out to your drink.

While enjoying your drink, drop back until you're perched on the edge of the stool, with your knees slightly bent. Adjust your weight distribution until it is even on both feet.

Step 3. Square your hips and shoulders to the bar.

If the bar or table is curved, use your foot line as a reference point. Bring your hips and shoulders into square with your feet.

Step 4. Wait for your drink to arrive.

Step 5. Lean forward from the hips and pay.

Step 6. Grasp your drink and lower yourself into an athletic position on the edge of the stool.

Bend your knees slightly until you are sitting just on the edge of the stool. Rest your weight more on the inside balls of your feet than on the stool.

Step 7. Adjust your weight distribution as necessary.

Feel yourself centered over the inside balls of both feet. Be sure that you are balanced.

Step 8. Drink your beverage.

Step 9. Repeat Steps 1 through 8 until happy hour has ended or proper weight distribution is instinctual.

Alcoholic beverages may affect your balance. Depending on your tolerance, you should either switch to nonalcoholic beverages or use your faltering equilibrium to solidify your practice of weight distribution.

PRACTICING PROPER KNEE PRESSURE WHILE DINING IN A RESTAURANT

The Cover: You are sitting and enjoying a meal out with a friend or spouse.

The Objective: To train proper knee pressure for your swing.

No one says that you cannot work on your golf swing while dining, but standing and setting up a shot in a restaurant as the server brings your meal may be catastrophic. The following steps work in a seated position with your hands under the table, so you won't risk knocking anything over, and no one will be the wiser.

The Gear:
- A table with a knee-length tablecloth
- A chair

The Technique:
Step 1. Position yourself at the table.

Sit facing the table so that your knees are tucked under the tablecloth. Adjust the tablecloth if necessary so that it runs across the center of your thighs. Tuck your butt back into the chair back so that your posture is upright. Place your feet flat on the floor about shoulder-width apart.

Step 2. Examine the menu.

Step 3. Place your hands under the table and make two fists.

Curl your fingers into your palms and wrap your thumbs around the fronts of your fingers.

Step 4. Place your fists together between your knees.

Press your hands together so that the sides of the fists touch, thumb to thumb and index finger to index finger. Straighten your arms in front of you until both of your fists are between your knees. You may have to lean forward slightly to achieve this—if so, take an interest in what your dining partner is saying.

Step 5. Squeeze your fists between your knees.

Focus on keeping an even pressure across your knuckles. Press your knees slightly toward each other so that your fists press together.

Step 6. Adjust pressure and direction as necessary.

During this dining exercise—and your golf swing—your knees should be pressing slightly toward one another. If your fists are slipping off each other, lighten the pressure and then push your knees straight into each other. Hold this evenly for a count of ten.

Placing your fists between your knees to test knee pressure forces you to lean forward slightly. Your companion will happily assume that you're listening attentively.

Step 7. Repeat Steps 1 through 6 throughout dinner every time you need to reach for your napkin or you want to appear more attentive.

Continue through dessert if more training is required.

CHAPTER 3

BACKSWING MOTION

PROPER BACKSWING MOTION

Backswing motion is essential to setting up and delivering the clubface squarely to the ball. Without a correct backswing motion, your swing will never be on the correct plane. Everything you have done up to this point with your grip, aim, and setup should add to your confidence to begin your backswing motion on the correct plane.

It's useful to practice your backswing motion on the course—generally just before you swing your clubs or start your round—but you will be in a much stronger position if you train your motion before you arrive at your 150-yard (137-m) recovery shot on the first hole. Preparing your backswing motion while sweeping, adjusting an overhead lamp, or standing in a doorway and talking to a coworker will lead you to a consistent routine and correct motion on the links.

The trajectory you want the ball to travel is established, in part, by the plane on which you start your backswing motion. A backswing that sets the club across the target line rather than parallel to it will set up a sweep that travels to the left or right of the line, causing a slice or a hook. Furthermore, a faulty backswing will create a chain reaction of errors that will carry through your downswing and finish (see Chapter 4).

When backswing motion begins or ends problem-
atically, your downswing motion will be both inaccurate
and stilted. Starting your takeaway with your hands or
arms will ensure that your club ends up either inside or
outside the target line. When started inside, the club will
return to the ball outside the target line and hook the
ball. Once started outside, the club will return to the ball
inside the target line and slice the ball. Failing to transfer
your weight to your right leg raises the height of impact
by raising the low point of your swing. This sets you up
to "top" the ball (your clubhead will hit the top of the ball
rather than below its midpoint). Swaying rather than
turning into your right hip socket will move the low point
in your swing forward or backward and will set you up
to hit too far down on the ball.

Check your backswing motion against the fundamentals listed below. While hugging a significant other,
sweeping, or swinging kids around, train your backswing
motion to begin with your core (see page 69). Train at
home, work, or when running errands to guarantee that
your responsibilities are tended to *and* your takeaway is
solid, straight, and instinctual.

Backswing Goals

- To turn so that, at the top of your backswing motion, the shaft of the club is parallel to the target line.

- To transfer your weight to your right leg, allowing you to set up a correct downswing motion and finish.

The Core

The "core" is the triangle formed by your left hip socket, your right hip socket, and the base of your sternum.

Backswing Elements

- Turn with the core to ensure a smooth takeaway.

  Use your big muscles (torso, back) rather than your arms and hands to turn away from the ball.

  Move your torso, arms, and hands together.

  Take the club straight back along the target line.

- Turn into your right hip socket while transferring your weight to your right leg.

  Your right hip should sit over your right leg—hips should not sway laterally.

  Your right knee should be slightly bent.

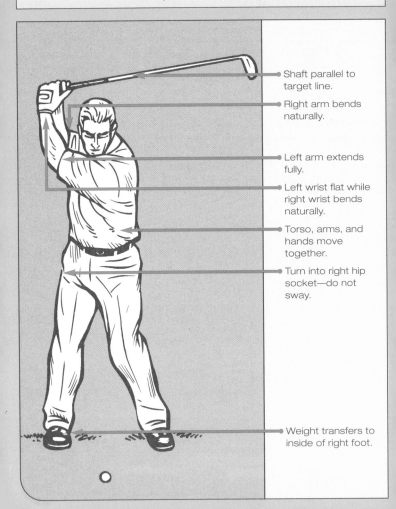

Shaft parallel to target line.

Right arm bends naturally.

Left arm extends fully.

Left wrist flat while right wrist bends naturally.

Torso, arms, and hands move together.

Turn into right hip socket—do not sway.

Weight transfers to inside of right foot.

Your weight should transfer to the right socket and the inside of your right foot.

- Keep arms in correct position.

    "Long" left arm should extend as far as it can.

    Right arm should bend naturally, as if it were connected to your right hip when you turn back.

    Right arm should bend to a 90-degree angle at the top of your backswing.

    Right elbow should point straight down to the ground.

    Your right and left thumb should point up as your right arm bends.

- Keep wrists in correct position at the top of the backswing.

    Keep left wrist flat, not cupped or bowed.

    Keep right wrist bent naturally under the club.

- Keep club shaft parallel to target line.

CHECKING YOUR STANCE FOUNDATION WHILE STANDING IN A DOORWAY

The Cover: You are chatting with a coworker while standing in his or her office doorway.

The Objective: To check your stance foundation prior to your backswing.

A correct backswing motion is executed by turning with the core into your right hip socket, thus setting your weight on your right leg. Shifting your weight laterally—i.e., swaying—to your right leg will not help your golf swing. Swaying shifts your plane back and leads to either a hook or a slice. Practicing your turn while standing in a doorway makes it impossible to sway—you'll hit the doorframe with your hip or shoulder.

The Gear:
- A standard-width doorway, 30–36 inches (75–90 cm) wide

- A coworker

The Technique:
Step 1. Stand in the middle of the doorway with your feet about shoulder-width apart.

Use the threshold of the doorway as your stance line—i.e., the line parallel to your imaginary target line—and set your feet on it.

Turn with your core to begin your backswing motion. Use the threshold of the door as a boundary; do not sway in or out of it.

Step 2. Square your hips and shoulders to the doorway.

Set your hips and shoulders square to the stance line. You will appear to be adjusting your position to better face your coworker.

Step 3. Straighten your back and bend your knees slightly to assume an athletic posture.

Lean forward from the hips and let your arms hang freely at your sides. Turn your head from side to side briefly, as if you were looking for something or someone down the hall—this will set up your cover for Step 4.

Step 4. Turn with the core to begin your backswing motion.

As you turn into your right hip socket, be sure that your right knee does not hit the side of the doorframe. Let your arms continue to hang freely at your sides and naturally follow your torso as it turns. Pretend to be searching for something or someone.

Step 5. Adjust your turn and conversation as necessary.

If adjustments to your turn are necessary, focus on turning within the frame of the door—i.e., around your right hip rather than across or toward it. If adjustments to your conversation are necessary, begin to speak about office gossip so that you naturally need to look over your shoulder to watch your back.

Stretching Your Legs While Talking on the Phone

On the days you plan on a long lunch/short nine holes, use your time in the office to warm up. Make a phone call, tuck the phone in between your ear and shoulder, and follow these steps:

1. Lower yourself onto one knee with your other leg in front, foot flat on the floor, as if you were proposing marriage.

2. Set your palms down on the floor, as if set up to sprint; your hands will remain flat on the floor throughout this exercise.

3. Slowly raise your butt upward.

4. Straighten your back leg as you rise up.

5. Slowly straighten your front leg as much as you comfortably can to stretch your front leg hamstring.

6. Stretch for 10 seconds and then repeat for opposite leg.

PRACTICING INSIDE ARM/KNEE PRESSURE WHILE HUGGING

The Cover: You are hugging a loved one.

The Objective: To perfect your inside arm and knee pressure.

A compact and correct golf swing requires that you keep a slight pressure inward at the armpits and knees. A meaningful hug delivered from you to a significant other incorporates the same pressure. Train your golf pressure and share the love as frequently as possible.

The Gear:
• A significant other—preferably shorter and more narrow than you

The Technique:
Step 1. Approach your significant other.

Smile and be amicable. Be the first to open your arms so that they are uppermost and outermost during the hug.

Step 2. Close your arms around your significant other at about shoulder level.

Intertwined arms are not recommended for this exercise.

Greet or say goodbye to a loved one with a great bear hug, in which you squeeze with your knees, arms, and chest. You'll be practicing your inside arm and knee pressure while conveying your affection.

Step 3. Begin to apply inward pressure at the arms and chest.

Apply an inward pressure from your armpits toward your chest. During both a correct golf swing motion and a hug, you should feel as though your arms and chest are connected about halfway down your pectoral muscles to about a third of the way down your biceps. Depending on the width of your significant other, you may have to lower your elbows to achieve this.

Step 4. Move in closer and position your knees.

Continue to apply pressure at the arms and chest and pull your significant other closer to you. Position your knees just to the outside—again, depending on the build of your significant other you may need to bend slightly at the knees to achieve this.

Step 5. Apply gentle inward pressure at the knees.

Press your knees toward each other with the knees of your significant other between. Feel the correct inward knee pressure that you should have throughout your golf swing. As the hug continues, you may need to offer positive reinforcement to your significant other to remain in this position—"mmm," "aah," and "I love you" are effective cues.

Step 6. Release pressure—and your significant other—and repeat as necessary.

Letting Go of Good and Bad Shots While Arguing with Your Significant Other

Whether letting go of a bad shot on the links or a past issue with your significant other, the keys are the same: express your feelings, relax, and focus on the present. Use the following techniques to improve your ability to "get over it," on the course and off.

- Verbally express your feelings. Nothing is gained by holding in or burying emotions. If you are hurt that you cannot go golfing, be hurt. If you are angry that you double-bogeyed the last hole, be angry. The only way to rid yourself of these feelings is to let them flow through you—and then go golfing.

- Once you have expressed your emotions, relax. Breathe in through the nose and out through the mouth.

- Know that no one is perfect. Every relationship—whether husband and wife, girlfriend and boyfriend, or golfer and golf club—is imperfect. You are bound to make mistakes. Simply recognizing your own and others' imperfections will allow you to accept things as they are.

- Focus on the present. Once you have expressed yourself, deal only with the issues at hand. There is nothing you can do about either a sliced drive on the last hole or your girlfriend flirting with another man several months ago. Look to the future and resolve to react differently.

TURNING YOUR CORE
WHILE SWEEPING

The Cover: You are sweeping the kitchen, dining room, or garage of debris.

The Objective: To work on starting your turn with the core.

Use the instructions that follow to tidy up both your initial turn and your floor.

The Gear:
- A common house broom, standard length
- A visibly dirty floor

The Technique:
Step 1. Determine where you will sweep your mess and draw your target line.

Choose an area about 2 feet (60 cm) to your left to make your pile. Place it central to the room so that it is accessible from all sides. Draw an imaginary line from the dirt to your target and stand so that your toes are along a line parallel to your target line. The dirt you are about to sweep should be in the center of your stance.

Step 2. Square your hips and shoulders to the target line.

Assume an athletic posture by bending your knees slightly.

Step 3. Grip the broom to your chest.

Grasp the broom about 3 inches (7.5 cm) from the top. With your palms facing you, close your hands around the broom—right on top of left. Pull the end of the broom to your chest so that your hands touch your sternum. Tuck your elbows to your sides and hold the broom in this position throughout the following steps.

Step 4. Set the broom down behind your pile.

Lean forward from the hips with a straight back and slightly bend your knees to lower the broom into position. The bristles of the broom should be perpendicular to and centered on your target line. If the bristles do not touch the floor, drop your hands slightly.

Step 5. Begin your backswing motion by turning your core into your right hip socket.

Your torso, arms, and hands will all move the broom back together. Keep your right knee flexed and stable— do not sway your hips. Keep your head down directly over your mess. Transfer your weight to your right leg as you turn and take the broom back along the target line. Turn only as far as you can while keeping the widest portion of the broom perpendicular to the target line.

Grasp the broom with your palms facing toward you and tuck your elbows to your sides. Lean forward until the broom is behind the pile of dirt you wish to sweep.

Keep your head steady as you bring the broom back along the target line, turning from the core (indicated with the dashed line). Sweep the dirt into the dustpan. Continue around the room until the floor shines.

Step 6. Return the broom to the position in Step 4.

Turn from the core (torso, arms, and hands together) to return the broom to your original position, centered on your pile. As you return, be sure that the broom contacts the floor and pushes your pile along the target line. Do not focus on anything more than turning back from the core—remember, this technique is to train your backswing motion and not your downswing or follow-through.

Step 7. Repeat Steps 1 through 6, adjusting your position to the pile and the target area as necessary.

Continue until you turn from the core every time you take the broom back and the room is completely swept.

CHECKING YOUR ARM POSITION WHILE MOVING AN ADJUSTABLE-ARM LAMP

The Cover: You are rearranging your adjustable lamp to take strain off your eyes.

The Objective: To check your arm position at the top of your swing.

Correct arm position at the top of your swing ensures that your club is parallel to your target line. Adjust your desk lamp to confirm that your arms are in the right position at the top of your backswing—and to ensure that your office or home office is properly lit.

The Gear:
- A chair

- A desk

- An adjustable-arm desk lamp

The Technique:
Step 1. Position yourself in your chair at your desk.

Sit so that the lamp is to your right and just above your head—between your right ear and right shoulder. The lamp should be about half an arm's length from where you are sitting.

Turn from the core while sitting—at the top of your "backswing" your hands and arms, if correctly positioned, will reach an adjustable lamp. Shine the light onto your workspace to soothe tired eyes.

Step 2. Adopt an athletic, seated posture.

With your feet flat on the floor, press your hips squarely into the seat back. Sit up straight and extend your spine from the base of your back to the crown of your head.

Step 3. Examine the lighting on your desk to determine how to adjust it.

Aim to adjust the light so that it casts shadows away from your work area or casts light just above your computer screen to diminish glare.

Step 4. Extend your arms in front of you at a 45-degree angle to the floor and grip an imaginary club just above your knees.

See "Checking Proper Hand Position in a Meeting" (page 30) for more detailed instruction. Your left arm should be straight and your right arm will be bent slightly at the elbow (toward your lap). Your hands will grip each other.

Step 5. Look at a spot on the desk about 12 inches (30 cm) in front of you.

Step 6. Turn from the core until your left shoulder is underneath your chin and your hands can reach the lamp.

Keep a long left arm as you turn and let your right arm fold naturally at the elbow, orienting your thumbs up.

Step 7. Check your arm position.

Turn at the neck to see your right arm position. A correct right arm at this point in your backswing is folded 90 degrees, with your elbow pointing at the ground.

Step 8. Adjust your right arm position and lamp.

Lower your left arm by simply letting it drop. Keep your torso and right arm in the position you arrived in for Step 6. Move your right arm if necessary so that it is in the correct position as described in Step 7. Extend your right hand and adjust the lamp.

Step 9. Repeat Steps 1 through 8 until your light is adjusted and your right arm consistently takes to the correct position.

Warm Up Your Arms While Hammering

When you need to finish a fix-it project or hang a picture before you hit the links, warm up your upper body muscles while you are hammering. Use at least a 12-ounce (336-g) hammer and follow these procedures with both arms for ten repetitions each.

Upward Exercise:

1. Grip the hammer so that it is upright with the head pointing away from you.

2. Tuck your elbow into your hip so that your forearm is parallel to the ground.

3. Bending from the wrist, lower the hammer straight down and then straight up (to its starting position, shaft perpendicular to the ground).

Backward Exercise:

1. Grip the hammer so that it is upside down with the head pointing toward you.

2. Tuck your elbow into your hip so that your forearm is parallel to the ground.

3. Bending from the wrist, touch the head of the hammer to your forearm and then return it to your starting position.

Side-to-Side Exercise:

1. Grip the hammer so that it is upright with the head pointing away from you.

2. Tuck your elbow into your hip so that your forearm is parallel to the ground.

3. Rotate your wrist and forearm to the left until the shaft of the hammer is parallel to the floor.

4. Rotate your wrist and forearm to the right until the shaft of the hammer is parallel to the floor.

CHAPTER 4

DOWNSWING MOTION AND FINISH

PROPER DOWNSWING MOTION AND FINISH

The downswing motion and finish are the final steps you must properly execute to deliver the clubhead squarely to the ball. Confidence in your downswing motion and finish will help you to complete your swing.

Your job is to begin the finishing motion correctly, allowing your body to release the clubhead (and thus the ball) on the trajectory you have previously established. The downswing is an exact mirror image of the backswing, and any misalignment will be reflected in ball flight.

The downswing motion and finish are the cumulative effects of your grip, aim and setup, and backswing motion. A downswing that starts by throwing or casting your hands at the ball will result in a topped or sliced shot. A downswing that is racked with tension will inhibit your ball flight and the natural momentum of the club.

Downswing motion and finish should be practiced on the lesson tee—and once or twice just before you address the ball. But you can also gain consistency and assurance by training in the everyday world. Gain trust in your downswing motion and finish while you swing kids around, shake hands at a convention, or just stand in line for a restroom. The key as you train to complete your swing is to trust the process.

Revisit the following fundamentals of downswing motion and finish and check your own routine against these basics. Practice starting with your core while at the water cooler. Train your head to stay steady while shopping for groceries. Confirm that your downswing motion and finish is a mirror image of your backswing motion, and when you arrive on the first tee you'll swing with confidence.

Downswing Motion and Finish Goals

- To allow the clubhead to complete the swing with its own force (using the laws of nature).

- To allow your body to follow the clubhead through the swing after impact.

Downswing Motion and Finish Elements

- Start with the core, turning your weight into the left hip socket.

  Rotate your core back toward the target.

  The clubhead should fall on the plane established by the backswing.

- Weight transfers into your left hip socket.

  Knees should be flexed and pressed inward.

  Body should stand up naturally once the core turns into left hip socket immediately after the moment of impact.

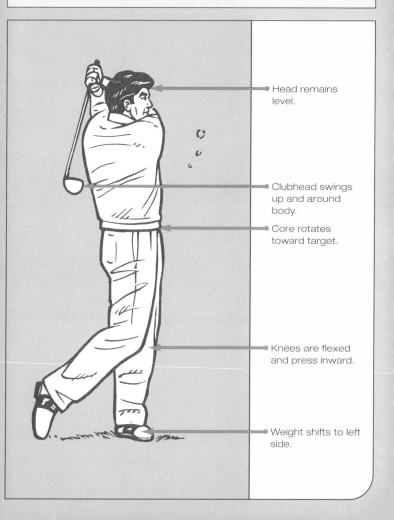

Head remains level.

Clubhead swings up and around body.

Core rotates toward target.

Knees are flexed and press inward.

Weight shifts to left side.

Weight shifts completely off right side.

- Club is free to follow the target line.

  Left arm remains long, up to hip high.

  Right arm follows clubhead out to target.

- Head remains level and behind the ball through down-swing.

- Body holds an even and balanced finish.

  Clubhead continues up and around body.

  Long left arm goes to hip high and then folds upward once past hip height.

  Your thumbs point up as your left arm folds.

  Head stays down until right shoulder naturally raises it.

  Right knee touches left knee when weight transfers to left hip socket.

  Right shoulder is left of the target.

STARTING WITH YOUR CORE WHILE AT THE WATER COOLER

The Cover: You are making friends with coworkers by serving them at the water cooler.

The Objective: To practice starting with your core.

With proper timing and structure, the office water cooler can be the perfect setting to practice starting your downswing motion with your core—and to get caught up on office gossip.

The Gear:
- A water cooler

- Two or more coworkers

The Technique:
Step 1. Position yourself in front of the water cooler.

Stand directly in front of the water cooler so only you have access to the cups and the spout.

Step 2. Ask two coworkers who are waiting for water to position themselves about an arm's length away, one directly to your left and the other directly to your right, so that you can get them their water.

Keep up a steady stream of "patter" so that they do not interrupt to ask why they must stand this way.

Practice your downswing motion and finish by swinging a cup of water from the water cooler to a thirsty coworker. Keep your arms straight and along the target line and, once you're on the course, your ball is sure to go straight.

Step 3. Take your stance.

Place your feet about shoulder-width apart, facing the water cooler. Square your hips and shoulders to the cooler. Straighten your spine and lean forward toward the spout as you bend slightly at the knees.

Step 4. Take a cup from the holder.

Step 5. Fill the cup with water.

Hold the cup under the spout with your right hand and activate the spout with your left. Keep your left arm long and your right arm slightly bent at the elbow as you fill the cup. Adjust your position back from the cooler if necessary to position your arms properly. Note the triangle formed by your outstretched arms.

Step 6. Turn to your right from the core and offer your coworker some water.

Grasp the water cup with both hands. Turn from the core as you set your weight into your right hip socket and take your arms (and the water) back. Keep a long left arm and let your right arm fold when your elbow reaches hip height. Stop your turn when you reach your coworker and hand her the water.

Step 7. Turn back to the cooler and repeat Step 5.

Step 8. When the cup is full, repeat Step 6.

As you turn from the core, feign surprise that the coworker to your right already has a cup of water. Apologize for your error.

Step 9. Starting from the core, turn your weight back into your left hip socket and hand your other coworker the water.

As you turn, keep a long left arm. Lead with your core and let your arms follow. Extend the water with your right arm as your weight sets into your left hip socket— let your left arm fold at the elbow when it reaches about hip height. Hand the water to your coworker.

Step 10. Repeat Steps 1 through 9 as needed.

Practicing Zen Mind
While Sipping Coffee

To golf effectively, you must be of sound mind. And that mind must be focused on only one thing—the task at hand. Whether tightening your golf shoe spikes, watching the fresh dew evaporate off the fairway, or driving a 250-yard (228-meter) carry over water, you must be present in each event. Such a mindset is commonly referred to as "Zen mind." While sipping coffee, use the following procedure to train your Zen mind before stepping onto the links.

- Stand near the cup of coffee. Breathe in through the nose and out through the mouth. Watch as the steam rises and evaporates into the air.

- Prepare to pick up the cup of coffee, being mindful of which hand you are about to use. Insert a few fingers into the handle (if applicable), grasp, and slowly raise the cup to your mouth.

- Breathing in through the nose and blowing out through the mouth, deliver a few even puffs of air to cool the surface temperature of the coffee. Notice the aroma of the brew as you inhale.

- Raise the cup to your lips. Consciously and carefully tilt the cup until the liquid passes your lips. Taste the coffee as it passes over your tongue.

- Set the cup down. Repeat to gain focus.

Note: As you sip your coffee, you may notice any of the following thoughts entering your mind: "This coffee would taste good on the golf course" or "what does coffee have to do with my golf game?" or "when is my tee time?" If any thought—other than a thought about the present moment—enters your mind, simply notice it. Watch it as it "passes by," but do not attach meaning to it or begin thinking about it. Stay focused on the task at hand: sipping coffee. Employ this technique on the golf course to remain focused and present.

KEEPING YOUR HEAD STEADY WHILE SHOPPING FOR GROCERIES

The Cover: You are completing your grocery shopping for the week.

The Objective: To keep your head steady.

A steady head is essential to your golf swing, but remember that the common instruction to "keep your head down" is a bit misleading. Your head should stay steady as you keep your eyes on the ball, but your chin must be clear of your shoulders to complete your back- and downswing motions. Practice keeping your head steady as you shop for groceries to confirm a sound head position.

The Setting:
• A grocery store aisle

The Gear:
• A shopping cart

The Technique:
Step 1. Stand in the aisle with your cart about 3 feet (1 m) in front of you and the shelves to your left about one arm's length away.

Step 2. Choose an item to take off the shelf to your left.

Select an item on a shelf about chest high.

Step 3. Take your stance.

Stand perpendicular to the shelves with your feet about shoulder-width apart. Square your hips and shoulders to your feet. Lean forward from the hips and bend your knees slightly.

Step 4. Focus on a spot on the floor and tuck your arms to your sides.

Choose a spot on the floor about 1 or 2 feet (30–60 cm) in front of you. This will be your "ball." Tuck your arms loosely to your sides so that your biceps contact the sides of your chest.

Step 5. Rotate from the core to your right.

Turn from the core to set your weight into your right hip socket. As you turn, keep your head steady and your eyes on your "ball." Continue to turn until your back is to the shelves on your left and your left shoulder is tucked under your chin. Keep your spine extended so your shoulder has room to move unimpeded under your chin.

When grocery shopping, keep your head steady and grasp items at the top of your downswing.

Step 6. Rotate from the core to your left.

Set your weight into your left hip socket and turn with the core back toward your grocery item. Reach out with your right arm and hand to grasp the item as you transfer your weight off your right side. Keep your head steady as you reach for the object—stay focused on your "ball" and let your shoulders turn around your spine.

Step 7. Grasp your item with your right hand.

As you complete your downswing motion, you should be close enough to grasp the item. Be sure that your right shoulder tucks under your chin. Let the motion of your shoulder carry your head upward to see that you have grasped the correct item—if so, place the item in your cart.

Step 8. Repeat Steps 1 through 7 until your shopping is complete or your head is consistently steady.

USING CENTRIPETAL FORCE AND GRAVITY WHILE SWINGING A KID AROUND

The Cover: You are entertaining a young child by swinging her around in a circle.

The Objective: To learn how to use centripetal force and gravity to complete your downswing motion and finish.

With the proper grip, aim and setup, and backswing motion in place, the laws of nature will complete your downswing motion and finish. In a proper swing gravity brings the clubhead to the ground, and thus to the ball. Centripetal force is responsible for carrying the clubhead around your core (the center of the circle), and thus on a plane. The same forces come into play when swinging a child around. Use the following off-course procedure to familiarize yourself with these forces while performing a solid downswing motion and finish.

Centripetal force is "center seeking." This means that the force is directed to the center of the circle. It is the force applied when, for example, you swing a rope with a weight attached to one end.

Grip the child under her armpits and take your stance. Set your feet shoulder-width apart along a line. Lean forward from the hips and slightly bend your knees.

Turn from the core as you swing the child from side to side, keeping your arms straight and in position along the backswing and downswing.

The Gear:
- A child at least three years of age and weighing under 50 pounds (23 kg)

The Technique:
Step 1. Pick up the child.

Turn the child to face you and grasp her under her armpits with your hands. Tuck your arms to your sides so that your elbows touch your hips. Pick up and set down the child several times to test her weight and her willingness to play. Lift the child and straighten your arms fully before proceeding to Step 2.

Step 2. Swing the child around in a circle about hip high.

Spin her around so that you are the center of the circle, keeping your position steady. The faster you turn, the higher the child's legs will rise in the air and the more centripetal force you are using. Notice the pull you feel from the center of the circle toward the end of the child. This is the same force (though to a lesser extent) you should feel from your grip (and core) toward the club-head as you swing. Add an audible "wheeee" as you turn to distract any onlookers or participants from the fact that you're practicing your golf swing.

Step 3. Stop turning and set the child down directly in front of you.

Step 4. Take your stance.

Set your feet about shoulder-width apart on a line. Square your hips and shoulders to the line. Visualize a target line parallel to and about 1 foot (30 cm) in front of the first line.

Step 5. Regrip the child.

Lean forward from the hips and bend slightly at the knees as you pick up the child as described in Step 1.

Step 6. Turn from the core to your right.

Take the child straight back along the target line as you set your weight into your right hip socket. Do not attempt to make a full backswing motion with the child. Turn only as far as you can while keeping both arms straight and long and the child on the target line. Feel the force as you turn.

Step 7. Turn from the core to your left.

Clear your hips as you set your weight into your left hip socket. This will ensure that the child will travel straight down the target line. Do not force the child back down the target line as you turn. Let gravity and the motion of your body move her down and through. This is the same force that will carry your clubhead down and through the ball.

Step 8. Repeat Steps 1 through 7 as necessary until you are familiar with using centripetal force to complete your downswing.

Repeat with other available children so that no one feels left out.

CHECKING YOUR ARM TRIANGLE WHILE MOPPING

The Cover: You are cleaning your dining room, kitchen, or bathroom floors.

The Objective: To check your arm triangle.

By now you are familiar with the core—the triangle formed by your hips and sternum. You should next familiarize yourself with the secondary triangle formed by your shoulders and hands. This triangle should be consistent at the beginning of your backswing (prior to bending your right arm), at impact, and at the beginning of your finish motion (prior to bending your left arm). A similar triangle may be formed with an adjusted grip on a wet mop. Clean your floors—and clean up your swing—at least once a week.

The Gear:
- A wet string mop

- A hardwood, tile, or linoleum floor

- A bucket of warm water with soap or other cleaner

The Technique:
Step 1. Dip the mop into the water and squeeze out extraneous water.

Cleaning the bathroom floors is an easy way to please your housemates and check the triangle formed between your two shoulders and your grip.

Step 2. Grip the mop.

Grip the mop with a full grip. Depending on the thickness of the mop handle, you may have to grip down closer to its center of gravity to get a solid hold on the tool.

Step 3. Take your stance and select a target line.

Select a spot to your right to be mopped. Visualize a target line that intersects the spot. With your feet about shoulder-width apart, stand on a line parallel to your target line. Stand far enough back so that the mop travels along the target line as you move it. Square your hips and shoulders to the target line.

Step 4. Set the mop—centered in your stance—on the area to be cleaned.

Lean forward from the hips and bend slightly at the knees so the mop touches the floor. Your hands should be slightly in front of—or even with—the area to be cleaned. Note the triangle formed by your shoulders and hands. Your goal is to keep this triangle intact throughout your mopping motion.

Step 5. Turn to your right with the core.

Take the mop back along the target line as you set your weight into your right hip socket. Turn only as far as you can while keeping the mop on the target line. The mop will lift up off the floor. If it moves inside or outside the target line or your right arm begins to bend, you have turned too far for this exercise.

Step 6. Turn to your left with the core.

Return the mop down and through the area to be cleaned as you set your weight into your left hip socket. Move your core through the impact area first and allow the laws of nature to return the mop along its path (see "Using Centripetal Force and Gravity While Swinging a Kid Around," page 105). Keep a long left arm and be sure your hands do not get in front of or behind the mop as you move the mop down the target line. Turn only as far as you can while keeping the mop on the target line. If the mop moves inside or outside the target line, or your left arm begins to bend, you have turned too far for this exercise.

Step 7. Check your triangle and the area to be cleaned.

Hold your finish position and check to be sure that the triangle formed by your shoulders and hands is intact. Check the mop head to be sure that it is on, not inside or outside, the target line. Check that the area to be cleaned is clean.

Step 8. Repeat Steps 1 through 7, moving around the room until the floor sparkles and your triangle remains intact both back and through your partial swing.

SWINGING TO THE TARGET WHILE SHAKING HANDS AT A CONVENTION

The Cover: You are shaking hands with business contacts at a convention.

The Objective: To swing your arms to the target instinctually.

Whatever your handicap, you need to know how to direct the ball toward your target. Whatever your business, you need to know how to network and make contacts at trade shows and conventions. Luckily, the motions for the two activities are one and the same. To improve your golf swing—and to build your career—use the following techniques.

The Gear:
• Two new acquaintances

The Technique:
Step 1. Position yourself between your two acquaintances.

Stand in a small cluster so that one is to your left and the other is to your right.

Step 2. Take your stance.

Stand with your feet about shoulder-width apart. Square your hips and shoulders to the line of your feet. Nod at both acquaintances as you prepare your position. Lean forward from the hips and bend your knees slightly.

Step 3. Raise your right hand into position.

Bend your arm at the elbow—about hip high—until your hand is in front of you ready to shake hands.

Step 4. Turn from the core to the acquaintance on your right.

Set your weight into your right hip socket as you turn with the core. Keep your arm in position while turning. Stop your turn when your back is to the acquaintance on your left and your right arm is in position to shake, still hip high. (Note: At this point in your movement, the palm of your right hand should be parallel to the target line.)

Step 5. Shake hands.

Make small talk as you feel the square and proper back-swing position of your right hand.

Position yourself between two colleagues and introduce yourself. Turn from the core to shake hands with each in turn, keeping your arms along the target line. Draw back to your right to prepare for your downswing motion and finish, which will put you in position to shake hands with the man to your left.

Step 6. Turn from the core to the acquaintance on your left.

Set your weight into your left hip socket as you turn. Be sure that, as you pass what would be your impact zone, your right hand and arm are still in the correct position. The palm of your right hand should be perpendicular to the line of your feet, hips, and shoulders.

Step 7. Continue to turn from the core toward the acquaintance on your left.

As you complete your turn, extend your right hand to meet your acquaintance's hand. Be sure that your palm carries down the target line. Note which company your acquaintance works for as your palm moves into parallel with your target line.

Step 8. Continue to shake hands with new acquaintances until the convention is over.

You will have significantly improved your business network and your ability to position your right hand at impact and follow-through.

PRACTICING YOUR RIGHT-KNEE-FORWARD FINISH WHILE STANDING IN LINE FOR THE BATHROOM

The Cover: You are waiting in line to use the bathroom.

The Objective: To perfect your right knee forward finish.

When you finish your golf swing, your legs will naturally turn so that the front of your right knee touches the inside of your left knee. You have completed your downswing and finish motion properly and come to rest in a natural, balanced position. Conveniently, this position mimics the stance one takes when the need to use the restroom is dire. Combining the practice of the right knee forward finish while waiting in line for the bathroom will draw little to no attention your way—you may, however, receive offers to step to the front of the line.

The Setting:
• A line to get into the bathroom (found most frequently at sporting events, movie theaters, conventions, and airports)

The Technique:

Step 1. Step into the line for the bathroom.

Stand perpendicular to the line so that one of your shoulders is to the back and the other is to the front of the line.

Step 2. Take your stance.

Set your feet about shoulder-width apart on an imaginary parallel line. Square your hips and shoulders to this line. Lean forward from the hips and bend your knees slightly. Let your arms hang freely at your sides.

Step 3. Turn from the core to set your weight into your right hip socket.

Move your torso, arms, and hands together as you turn toward the patron to your right. Express—either verbally or nonverbally—your discomfort at having to wait.

Step 4. Turn from the core to set your weight into your left hip socket.

Move your torso, arms, and hands together as you turn toward the patron to your left and complete your downswing motion. Be sure to finish your turn so that you completely face the patron on your left. Let your right knee come forward so that the natural finish of your turn raises your right heel.

When you complete your downswing motion and finish your weight will be set into your left hip socket and your right knee will come forward toward your left. Others in line for the bathroom with you will never suspect you're practicing your golf swing.

Step 5. Hold this position.

With your weight on your left leg, feel and hold this balanced position for a count of ten. Note that this is the position you will be in when you complete a solid, balanced golf swing. If you notice onlookers worrying about your condition, shift quickly from side to side to indicate that you have control over the situation.

Step 6. Move forward in line as necessary and repeat Steps 1 through 5 until it's your turn to use the facilities.

CHAPTER 5

PUTTING

THERE IS NO PROPER PUTTING TECHNIQUE

Putting is as essential to your golf game as a sound and repeatable swing motion. There is, however, no one proper way to putt. Thus, the practice of putting is a unique procedure for each golfer—what works for one person may not work for another.

Putting is made up of two primary elements: speed and line. The former comes only from experience on the links or a home (or office) putting green. The latter, however, may be acquired both on and off the course. Find a grip, stance, and putter that work consistently for you and your style. Chances are, all three of these elements will come through trial and error.

Once you can consistently putt a ball on a line, the challenge is to find your target line and get the ball to roll on it. This involves being able to read the green, to see the line, and to deliver the clubface squarely to the ball.

There are numerous causes for failed putts. Your speed may be too great or too slight, causing the ball to run by or stop short of the hole. Your read may be off to the left or the right of the hole, causing you to stroke an effective putt down an ineffective target line. Your alignment may be inaccurate, causing your ball to roll down a well-read but incorrect target line. Your clubface may be open or closed at impact, causing the ball to go left or right of a well-read and accurate target line. The list goes on.

Instead of focusing on all the variables that could go wrong, focus on what can go right. Practice swinging your shoulders and hands while carrying shopping bags. Train yourself to read greens and terrain while hiking or taking a walk. Test your ability to read the grain of a green while vacuuming. These skills are vital off-course techniques you can use to arrive on the green and putt with confidence.

Putting Motion Goals

- To get the ball rolling on the correct target line.

- To put the ball into the hole.

Putting Motion Elements

- A comfortable grip (using any of the following):

    Right hand low.

    Left hand low.

    The claw.

- A firm grip pressure, soft enough to feel the weight of the clubhead.

- A solid and accurate read of the green.

    Recognition of the break.

    Recognition of the grain of the grass.

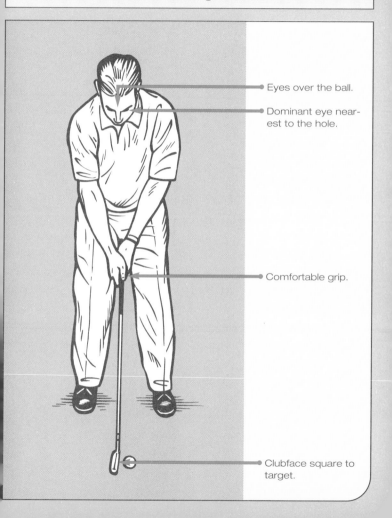

Eyes over the ball.

Dominant eye nearest to the hole.

Comfortable grip.

Clubface square to target.

Good judgment of necessary speed to deliver the
ball to the hole.

- A square alignment of the clubface to the target.

- Clear visibility of the target line.

   Eyes directly over the ball and target line.

   Dominant eye closest to hole.

- A smooth, accelerating stroke.

   Triangle formed by shoulders and grip stays
   constant.

   Head stays over the ball.

SWINGING THE PENDULUM WHILE SHOPPING

The Cover: You are helpfully volunteering to hold your significant other's bags while shopping.

The Objective: To work on swinging the pendulum.

When your hands grip your putter, a triangle is formed between your two shoulders and your grip. This triangle is responsible for your putting stroke. The triangle should move as a pendulum, making contact with the ball at the lowest point in the arc for a smooth and accelerating stroke. Practice your putting stroke as you walk with shopping bags to secure a solid putting motion.

The Gear:
• Three shopping bags with handles—about 2 to 3 pounds (1–1.5 kg) total weight

The Technique:
Step 1. Grasp the shopping bags in front of you.

Use both hands to hold the shopping bags together by the handles. The bags should be directly in front of you and clear of your legs. Bend your elbows slightly so your hands are about hip height.

Swinging bags along an imaginary target line simulates swinging your putter on the course.

Step 2. Select a target line.

Choose a target line in front of you. The target line should run on the floor just underneath the shopping bags. Depending on their size you may only be able to see the line in front of and behind the bags.

Step 3. Take your stance.

Using whatever putting stance you practice, stand so that you can both see the line and settle your eyes directly over it. Your eyes and shoulders must be square to the line. Your feet and hips may be square or open to the line.

Step 4. Begin your backswing putting motion.

Rotate to the right from the shoulders so that your hands, arms, and shoulders all move together. Take the shopping bags straight back to the right along the target line. Depending on the weight of your bags, you may need to shift your triangle in the opposite direction to start your motion. Think of swinging a bucket full of sand. To keep the bucket level your hands would need to move slightly left before moving all the way back to your right. Go right only as far as you can while keeping the bags on the target line.

Step 5. Let the bags swing your triangle back and forth.

Let gravity swing the bags back and forth along the target line. The weight of the bags falling forward and backward should move your hands, arms, and shoulders together. Focus on separating the triangle from the rest of your body so that your body remains stationary as your hands, arms, and shoulders rotate around it. Be sure the bags remain on the target line.

Step 6. Repeat Steps 1 through 5 until you can consistently swing the pendulum or your significant other returns.

DETERMINING YOUR DOMINANT EYE WHILE WORKING OUT

The Cover: You are stretching your arms at the gym—and flirting with a stranger.

The Objective: To determine your dominant eye.

Putting with your dominant eye closest to the hole allows you to see the target line more clearly. Generally, right-handed people are left-eye dominant and vice versa. Some do putt better from their non-dominant-eye side, however. Use the following technique to determine which eye is dominant. This exercise is best performed at your gym, where you can pretend to be warming up while also checking out the scene.

The Gear:
• Your target—preferably someone you find attractive

• Your thumb

The Technique:
Step 1. Extend your dominant arm directly out in front of you.

Position yourself so that your arm is extended toward your target. Make a fist with your extended hand. Stretch your arm slightly as if you are warming up for your workout.

Step 2. Extend your thumb upward toward the ceiling.

With both eyes open, move your arm up and down or side to side until your thumb aligns just below the target in your line of vision. Exhale to "let off" steam and appear more natural as you stretch.

Step 3. Look past your thumb to the target.

Again keeping both eyes open, be sure that the target—and not your thumb—is in focus. Take a closer look at your potential date to determine if he is wearing a wedding ring.

Step 4. Alternate closing one eye at a time.

Hold each eye closed for about 1 second. Note the distance your thumb appears to move from alignment with the target.

Step 5. Repeat Steps 1 through 3 with your opposite arm.

Step 6. Determine your eye dominance.

If, when you held your right eye closed, your thumb appeared to move farther from your target, you are right-eye dominant. If, when you held your left eye closed, your thumb appeared to move farther from your target, you are left-eye dominant.

Step 7. Strike up a conversation with the target, if desired.

"Winking" at an attractive target will help you determine your dominant eye—and may get you a date.

READING GREENS WHILE VACUUMING

The Cover: You are meticulously vacuuming your carpet.

The Objective: To quickly read the grain of a green.

Your ability to determine the grain of a green will help you determine the speed of your putt. The most helpful rule is simple: Grass grows toward the sun. This means in the morning, putting easterly, you will be putting with the grain; putting westerly, you will be putting against the grain; and putting northerly or southerly, you will be putting across the grain. This rule is often negated, however, by foot traffic on the green. Use the following procedure while vacuuming to hone your reading skills.

The Gear:
- A vacuum

- A medium-pile carpet—no shag

The Technique:
Step 1. Lower yourself so that your eyes are just slightly above the carpet.

Look at the area you will be vacuuming and scan for extraneous dirt.

Step 2. Examine the grain of the carpet.

The darker areas on the carpet signify the back of the pile—this is equivalent to putting against the grain. The lighter areas on the carpet signify the front of the pile, or putting with the grain. (The same is true on the green: darker areas indicate that you're putting against the grain, and vice versa.)

Step 3. Note the consistency of the grain.

Most carpets will have areas that are both against and with the grain—places where people have scuffed their feet. Your goal is to level the grain of the carpet in the entire room.

Step 4. Begin to vacuum from one end of the room to the other.

Consistently vacuum either away from you or toward you—only in one direction. Pick up the vacuum when you finish a stroke and set it down next to the area you just vacuumed. Notice how the grain of the carpet of the line you vacuumed moves in the same direction. If the grain is not consistent, reset the vacuum to a lower pile height and repeat until the entire room is finished.

Step 5. Turn off the vacuum and set it aside.

Step 6. Walk in a random pattern around the room.

Remove your shoes so as not to soil the newly vacuumed surface or create more static electricity on the pile. Use variable steps—short, long, dragging, and skipping.

Meticulously vacuum your carpet so the pile faces the same direction, then walk around in a random path. Stop and take a look at the varying grain. Learn to identify when the carpet is laying with the grain or against it, and you'll be able to instinctually read the green during your next golf game.

Step 7. Stand in the center of the room and read the carpet.

From an upright position, you should be able to easily read the grain of your steps. Notice the lighter areas and darker areas and make a mental note of the corresponding grain of the carpet. Change your position in the room and reread the carpet. Focus on training your mind to register, "against the grain," or "with the grain," when you see dark or light patches, respectively.

Step 8. Repeat Steps 1 through 7 until reading the grain of your carpet is second nature or your entire house has been vacuumed.

Stretching Your Lower Back While Picking Up the House

When piles of clothing, newspaper, toys, or other household obstacles are physically affecting your ability to get out the door and onto the links, it's time to take charge. Use the following procedure to warm up and stretch your back muscles as you work your way out of the house, into your significant other's good graces, and on deck at the first hole.

Note: Do not use this procedure on any object greater than 10 pounds (4.5 kg).

1. Step up to the item that needs to be picked up.

2. Roll your torso down to the object by lowering your head, shoulders, upper back, and lower back in succession.

3. Let your arms fall to the object.

4. Grasp the object with one or two hands, as its weight requires.

5. Hold this position for a count of ten. Feel the backs of your legs, lower back, and neck muscles stretch as you bend over.

6. In succession, roll your lower back, upper back, shoulders, and head into an upright position as you lift the object.

7. Place the object on or in its appropriate shelf, container, or laundry basket.

8. Repeat until your home is tidy and your back is properly stretched.

READING TERRAIN WHILE HIKING

The Cover: You are taking in the beauty of nature while on a hike or walk in the park.

The Objective: To quickly read the grade of the terrain and assess your ball's path after landing.

When it comes to the break of the greens, remember that the green always breaks "downstream." In other words, a ball will naturally roll on the same path that water would run off the same surface. Your ability to putt effectively relies on your ability to read the green and thus choose an accurate line on which your ball will travel.

The Setting:
• A path to hike or walk

The Technique:
Step 1. Take note of the general landscape.

Before you begin your walk, examine the territory for high and low points. Look for the highest points (mountain peaks) and the lowest points (a pond, lake, or other drainage area). Walk in whatever area you desire, but always be aware of the changes in grade.

Pick a target and landing zone in the distance and determine which way water would flow if poured onto the zone. You'll learn to read terrain and predict your ball's path while enjoying the scenery.

Step 2. Choose a small flat area and walk toward it.

Choose an area about 100 yards (90 m) away—about the same distance you would be walking after hitting a sound approach shot. The area should be about 10–20 yards (9–18 meters) wide. This will be your "green."

Step 3. Study the tilt of the land leading to your makeshift green.

Just as you would when on the links, take note of the landscape leading up to the "green." Which way would water flow once it reached the area?

Step 4. Read the terrain of your makeshift green as you approach it.

Look for high points and low points on the area itself and, as in Step 3, imagine how water would flow at these points.

Step 5. Walk to the center of your "green" and read the terrain.

Using the read you gathered from Steps 3 and 4, study the terrain in relation to the land around it. Note the tilt of the green in relation to the larger landscape. If you are in a valley, the green will generally break away from the mountains. If you are in a flatland area or park, the green will always break toward the low point.

Step 6. Repeat Steps 1 through 5 until you can effectively and instinctively read greens or until you have completed your hike.

ACKNOWLEDGMENTS

Joe Borgenicht would like to thank his invaluable editor, Erin Slonaker. He would also like to give thanks to Dave Borgenicht, Mike Rogalski, Dan Krovatin, and the entire team at Quirk Books. If not for Grandma Helen (85 and still swinging) and the teachings of R. D. Robinson, Joe would never be as addicted to golf as he is. And finally he would like to acknowledge his soon-to-be golfing buddy for life, Jonah, and his wife, Melanie—thanks for trying.

R. D. Robinson gives heartfelt thanks to Ms. Joni of the University of Utah Dance Department, who led him down the path of teaching and working with people with disabilities. He would also like to thank his son Patrick for being the test case for a new swing motion, progressing from a beginner to scratch golfer in four years (not bad!)—he's made dad proud.

ABOUT THE ILLUSTRATOR

Dan Krovatin has worked for numerous clients in advertising, publishing, and editorial, most notably long stints for *Men's Health*, *Golf Digest*, and *Men's Fitness*. He lives and breathes in Ewing, NJ, with wife and daughter. After completing the illustrations for this book, he magically reduced his handicap by ten strokes.